Boghos Vartabed Natanian

FIRST REPORT ON
THE DIOCESE OF NICOMEDIA
1870

The Visitation Made by
Archimandrite (Vartabed) Boghos Natanian

Translated and annotated by
Ara Stepan Melkonian

Gomidas Institute
London

© Ara Stepan Melkonian 2019
ISBN 978-1-909382-50-3

For more information please visit our website (details below).
Gomidas Institute
42, Blythe Road,
London W14 0HA
United Kingdom
www.gomidas.org
info@gomidas.org

CONTENTS

Translator's Note   7
Acknowledgements   11
Preface   13
Bibliography   44

Part 1 The Main Part of the Diocese of Nicomedia*
Nicomedia   15
Dagh Kiugh   17
Armash   17
Khasgal   17
Almali   18
Fendekli   18
Ferizli   19
Tamlekh   19
Nor Kiugh   20
Adabazar   20
Geyve's Michakiugh   22
Kourdbelen   23
Kendjelar   23
Sabandja or Heghinoupolis†   24
Aslan Bey [Arslan Beg]   25
Ovadjek   26
Deongel   26
Bardizag   26

---

* This title was added to conform with the subsequent parts.
† Transliterated from Armenian.

Part 2 The Second Part of the Diocese of Nicomedia Consisting of the Armenian Villages in the Yalova Province

Shakhshakh	29
Kheledj Kiugh	29
Choukhour Kiugh	30
Kartsi Kiugh	30
Chengiler	31
Bazar's Medz Nor Kiugh	32
Bazar's Michakiugh	33
Bazar's Keremet	34
Yalakh Dere	35
Merdigeoz	36

Part 3 Description of wedding celebrations in the Armenian-inhabited-villages of the Yalova region

Betrothal	39
Inter-family Relationships	40
Marriage	41

ԱՌԱՋԻՆ

ՏԵՂԵԿԱԳՐՈՒԹԻՒՆ

ՎԻՃԱԿԻՆ ՆԻԿՈՄԻԴԻՈՅ

ԱԾԵԼՈՒԹԵՆԱՄԲ ՆԱԹԱՆԱԷԼ ՊՕՂՈՍ ՎԱՐԴԱՊԵՏԻ

Կ. ՊՕԼԻՍ
ՏՊԱԳՐՈՒԹԻՒՆ Գ. ՏԷՐՎԼԷՆԵԱՆ
)(1874)(

Translator's Note

This small book, published in Constantinople in 1871, is the result of the very first attempt at surveying the Armenian community of the Nicomedia area[*] since its foundation more than 300 years before.[†]

It was one of the several surveys made[‡] at the behest of the Armenian Apostolic Patriarchate of Constantinople,[**] during that time, of various areas in the Ottoman Empire with Armenian communities.

Archimandrite (*vartabed*) Boghos Natanian conducted this survey starting in September 1870. He completed and prepared it for publication by the end of March 1871 – a period of six months - having visited 28 towns and villages. It is probable that visits made to the smallest communities only lasted a day, while others lasted longer, especially if he felt obliged to intervene (as he did) in local affairs.

Bearing in mind the frequently severe winters in the area, he might have actually completed his mission by the middle of November 1870 – in about two months - then returned to Constantinople. There he would have spent considerable time collating and editing the notes he'd made prior to submitting the finished report to the patriarchal authorities and preparing it for print.

In my opinion this demonstrates how little information was

1. Held at the diocesan prelacy

2. Transmitted to the Armenian Apostolic Church's Patriarchate in Constantinople.[††]

---

[*] The term "area" is, in this context, synonymous with "diocese."
[†] There were no Armenian communities in the Nicomedia (Izmid) area before 1525.
[‡] They were made under similar conditions by Vahan Minakhorian and Bishop Karekin Srvantsiants.
[**] Hs Beatitude Archbishop Mgerdich Khrimian, later elected Catholicos of All Armenians as Mgerdich I.
[††] Records held in the villages and towns weren't always what they should have been; in most places the priest kept his own in whatever form he chose – or not accurately at all. It is questionable whether any were forwarded to the prelacy. It was probable also true that small villages especially were not considered to be of any importance by the various Armenian Patriarchate advisory and governing bodies at that time.

It is noticeable that some of the communities that the present generation of Armenians originating in the Nicomedia diocese know of, or are from, did not exist in 1870. Even some of the larger communities (such as Ovadjek) were still only villages at that time.

One must accept that when the author does not mention who the people of a particular village were, they must have been Armenians belonging to the Armenian Apostolic Church. In all other instances he is careful to state "Greek," "Turk," "Jewish," "Protestant," "Armenian-Hrom"* and "Papist" (Roman Catholic).

It is clear from the text that the author – an Armenian Apostolic Church cleric who was a Doctor of Theology (vartabed or archimandrite) – followed a set agenda, using the same criteria and even descriptive wording for each of the communities he visited.

An interesting aside in some of these is his note "the people here lack morals."† One is led to wonder what this meant, bearing the social conventions, date and his calling in mind.‡ Another is a certain bias against both Protestants and Armenian Catholics; in one place he states that the sending of Armenian Apostolic families' children to a Protestant school was "saddening and shameful!"

Judging by some of the notes he made, Natanian was able, thanks to his rank, the official documents he had and the respect that churchmen received at that time, to ask awkward questions concerning finance, schools, the clergy etc in the villages and towns he visited. He even conducted an examination of a married priest's conduct in one village and had a girls' school opened in another!

He must also have had a forceful personality that facilitated all this work and he didn't fail to point a finger at an Armenian who was using his position to steal money that belonged to the village he was 'ruling," or at an avaricious priest who was lending local people money at some rate

---

* Armenians of the Greek Orthodox faith.

† The expression used, when characterising the local people, was *paroyaganoutene zourg...*

‡ Community rules were very strict in those days; the separation of the sexes was the norm (except in the home) and parents were very protective of the morals and behaviour of the young as the 'good name' of the family was paramount.

of interest. It is also noticeable, in these instances that he refrained from taking any official action, merely reporting what he found.

In keeping with Middle Eastern custom and practice, one can see, again and again, how the schooling of boys was given much more emphasis than that of that of girls. Even that – apart from noteworthy exceptions – was poor, even if the village or town had been in existence for many years. Education, in many places, was very low on the villagers' list of priorities at that time. The "teachers" were often simply bookkeepers (*hamaradou*)[*] who had no real teacher training. One is left to wonder whether this report had any effect on the educational drive evident in the region subsequent years.

Of necessity the author made one big assumption: the average number of inhabitants of any one house was five individuals. Unfortunately, there were no real records or censuses available to him at that time, so a rough and ready benchmark number had to be determined.[†] The author, however, didn't always stick to this assumption, using population figures he must have obtained locally.

The language he used is based on classical Armenian but tended towards modern, western (Constantinople) dialect. It is reasonably easy to read, but he used words which perhaps do not embody the meaning he gave them. An example of this is the word *tankaran*, meaning museum; he used it to mean "meeting hall" or "lecture hall."[‡]

The distances Natanian quoted (in hours) between one village and another is the time taken – travelling on foot – to reach it from the one he started from.

It is to be noted that Natanian didn't give his sources; one can only assume that the material he used was verbal, written down by him at the time and collated later. The exception, of course, was the final part – the

---

[*] Hamaradou means accountant; in view of the position of the teacher in the villages bearing this title, I have opted for the lesser one, that of "bookkeeper."

[†] In my opinion this might be an underestimate, as many families had large numbers of children, as well as relatives, living in any one house in a patriarchal style at that time.

[‡] This particular meaning is gleaned from the text by inference. No dictionary, be it a contemporary, classical or modern Armenian publication, gives this meaning.

description of marriage etc customs in the Yalova area - which was clearly prepared by someone else and which was just added to the published work.

This survey should be compared to that prepared and presented by Minas Kasabian which was completed in 1913, 43 years later.[*] The differences in statistics dealing with similar places and subjects in the two works are astonishing![†] It would appear that the drift westward by Armenians from the eastern provinces of the Ottoman Empire to its capital continued, coupled with a high birth rate and the influx of Armenians from Ordu after 1875 who were known locally as "Laz Armenians."

* * * * *

The last part, the description of betrothal, relationships and marriages in the Yalova region, is a racy document written in the vernacular without any concessions to grammar or punctuation by someone who was not as well educated as Natanian. This second author writes in the present tense without any real sense of narrative and uses Turkish words in the text, probably because they were part of the local dialect. His descriptions of events (without providing details of any sort) are interesting: "debauchery" and "battlefield" are just two that may be mentioned.

There is no explanation as to why Natanian appended this description to his survey without editing it; we are, however, fortunate that it was, as otherwise we would not have that piece of important social information available now.[‡]

---

[*] Minas Kasabian, *Hayere Nikomedio Kavarin Mech* [The Armenians in the Province of Nicomedia], Azadamard Press, Bardizag, 1913. It took two years to complete!

[†] Having read the two surveys, it seems to me that Kasabian was at least acquainted with Natanian's 1871 book.

[‡] The description offered here from 1870 should be compared to that shown in Krikor Mkhalian, *Bardizag and Its People*, translated by Ara Stepan Melkonian, Gomidas Institute, London 2014, Appendix, pp. 462-464. The Bardizag rules date from 1864 – six years earlier!

Acknowledgements

I should like to thank two people for their encouragement and assistance: Ara Sarafian, my good friend and the director of the Gomidas Institute, London, who suggested that this would make an important contribution to our knowledge of the region; and my wife, Anne Melkonian, who has never ceased to give me encouragement in my efforts to make the Armenian original of any particular work available to those who cannot read our ancestral language.

Any errors in the translation of this work are, of course, solely my responsibility.

Ara Stepan Melkonian
Plymouth, Great Britain,
2019

Preface

On the orders of the (Armenian Apostolic) Patriarch Archbishop Mgerdich Khrimian and in accordance with his encyclical letter of authority (*gontag*) dated 10 September 1870, I set out on an official visit to the diocese of Nicomedia.

After staying at the prelacy[*] for two days, I began to visit the various communities[†] on 12th September. I first went to Nicomedia itself then to all the communities, recording all the information that I collected piece by piece here, for the attention of the Archbishop and Patriotic Patriarch and for the protective Central Administration as well as to inform our dear fellow-Armenians.

With prayers,
Archimandrite (vartabed) Boghos Natanian

March 31, 1871
Constantinople

---

[*] Situated in Nicomedia (Izmid).
[†] The author has used vidjagainots (sees).

Part 1

The Main Part of the Diocese of Nicomedia*

Nicomedia [Izmid]

This city on the Bay of Izmid which was called, in ancient times, the Bay of Astacus, is built on a small hill on its northern side, 18 hours distant from Uskudar and seven hours distant by steamship from Constantinople.† It consists of 2,382 houses, with four nationalities living in them: Armenians, Greeks, Turks and Jews.

The Armenians have their own separate quarter comprising 500 houses with almost 2,500 inhabitants.

It has a magnificent stone-built church dedicated to the Holy Mother of God, with a most beautiful baptismal font built of marble the like of which has never been seen before. It is located on the eastern side of the anteroom accessed from the right-hand apse. This church has five married priests: Reverends Aristages, Hagop, Haroutiun, Nerses and Mesrob. Two are former pupils of Armash.

They have a wonderful, sea-facing prelacy near the church made up of seven rooms. The church has a school for boys and one for girls, but they are very poor. Although they have an income of 10,000 kurush per annum, both schools are absolutely decrepit and the children who should attend are scattered here and there. Although the people protest about this, the members of the council take no notice; they have heard the protests so often that they just consider them as a usual complaint. The majority of the people are poor with only a few people being wealthy.

They have a cemetery near the sea of an area of about 30,000 square *gankouns*,‡ in which 20,000 martyrs were buried. They are always celebrated by the Armenian Apostolic Church there. There was an ancient stone-built church, now ruined and mostly levelled with the ground, whose arches are the only things showing that it existed.

---

* Including the town of Izmid.

† I have used Constantinople throughout this translation as that was its formal name then.

‡ A *gankoun* is about a cubit, a unit of length of between 16-18 inches or 40-55cm.

First Report on the Diocese of Nicomedia, 1870

The Greeks have a separate quarter of 150 houses in the town. They number, in total, 750 individuals. They have a church and a school which is progressing. They also have a monastery about a quarter of an hour from the town with a marvellous church dedicated to St Pantelimon, containing the saint's tomb which they assert is 1,500 years old. It is said that his body is in Europe, with only his right hand and three fingers remaining in this monastery. There is a well with sweet water near this tomb, which is considered to have healing properties.

The Turkish community consists of 1,400 houses and number 4,000.[*] They have about 25 large and small mosques as well as several schools which do not provide tuition; thus they are still in Egyptian darkness, although they are not fanatical. They live in harmony with the Christians; some are artisans and others farmers. They have few merchants. There is an office where a *mutasarif* pasha and his soldiers live.

The town has a large imperial dockyard, next to which is the magnificent government building,[†] said to be built on the site of the palace belonging to either Emperor Julian or Maximus.

Apart from these, there are 30 Protestant houses with about 120 inhabitants. They have a meeting hall and school and a preacher (missionary). The school is quite progressive.

There are also two Roman Catholic[‡] houses with about 20 exiles who don't have either a church or school. They have a priest by the name of Hovsep Ayvazian,[**] who governs them.

There are 20 or 30 Jewish houses in another separate quarter whose inhabitants number 120 individuals. They have one synagogue. They are middle class people.

---

[*] Using Natanian's assumption, this figure should be 7,000.
[†] Natanian uses the word *balad* (palace) here.
[‡] The word used here is *babagan* (papist).
[**] He returned to the Armenian Apostolic Church in 1876, assuming the rank of archimandrite (*vartabed*).

Dagh Kiugh[*]

This village is made up of 20 houses with 100 inhabitants. They have a church (*akhshab*)[†] dedicated to the Apparition of the Holy Cross with one married priest named Reverend Kaloust.

The village has a small school teaching the children basic reading.

The people are generally famers and are ignorant and poor.

Armash

This village is six hours distant north-east of Nicomedia.

It has a monastery dedicated to the Holy Mother of God which has its own boarding school. All the members of its order, the majority of the teachers in the diocese as well as educated married priests are former pupils who have graduated from this school.

The village has 190 houses and 1,000 inhabitants. It has two married priests, Reverends Garabed and Stepan.

The village does have its own school but, because of internal dissension and not having an established income, its teacher's salary is paid by the monastery. As the monastery is also in difficult financial straits due to the cost of building its church, the village school is neglected.

The villagers are generally farmers and are involved in sericulture, but lack morals.

Khasgal

This village has 80 houses and is one hour away, opposite Armash.

It is built on a high hill and has about 400 inhabitants.

It has a church dedicated to St James with a married priest named Reverend Arsen.

The village has a school which depends on funds provided by the church. It has 30 children who learn basic reading skills.

It has one Protestant and one Turkish house.

---

[*] *Kiugh* means village; I have retained the proper (Armenian) name for accuracy throughout this work.

[†] This term is unknown to me.

The villagers are farmers and are involved in sericulture. They are very poor.

Almali[*]

On a high hill three hours east of Khasgal, it has 40 houses with approximately 200 inhabitants. It has a beautiful small church dedicated to St Garabed and two married priests Reverends Hagop and Khoren. The church has its own poor school, dependent on funds from it. It has 30 pupils taught by an ordinary bookkeeper.[†] The majority of the people are farmers and are involved in sericulture. They are poor and ignorant.

Fendekli

The village is a beautifully located place half an hour from Almali. It is divided into three parts and its population of 250 houses consists of Armenians and Armenian-Hroms, of which 20 houses are real (Armenian Apostolic) Armenians numbering 80 individuals.

The latter have a small wooden church dedicated to St Garabed, the doors of which have been closed for two years as they don't have a married priest in residence. Although they did have one, named Reverend Simeon from Bardizag, he left having relinquished his calling and now wanders from place to place in the Bardizag area. This church apparently owns a capital sum of 5,000 kurush, but when I checked I found that it had disappeared a long time ago.

It has a small school with five pupils who are taught basic reading skills. It is left neglected, without any form of assistance.

The villagers are mainly farmers with a few individuals involved in sericulture. They are in an extremely poor situation.

The Armenian-Hroms consist of 244 houses with 1,140 inhabitants and have three magnificent churches each with a progressive school.

The people are generally farmers with a few individuals involved in sericulture. They are quite wealthy. They are all Armenians who, not knowing Greek, speak Armenian but are educated is Greek.

---

* Later called Almalou.
† The word used here and elsewhere is *hamardou* (accountant) but I have used the term bookkeeper in all instances.

The Main Part of the Diocese of Nicomedia

Both communities live together in great harmony; those seeing this are truly astonished.

Ferizli

Ferizli is an hour east of Fendekli, on a small hill. It has 150 houses with approximately 800 inhabitants. It has a wonderful church dedicated to the Holy Mother of God with two married priests, leading married priest (*avak kahana*) Reverend Boghos and Reverend Mardiros.

The church has a school for both sexes with about 100 girls and boys attending. They are taught by a teacher who is an Armash graduate. About 20 boys and 20 girls who study grammar and mathematics are making good progress. The school also has a well-maintained meeting hall* the profits of which, together with those of the church, maintain the school.

The people of the village, however, having got used to not having to worry, have become uncaring. They are farmers and are involved in sericulture.

Finally, it is very hard for patriotic hearts to see this community's indifference.

Tamlekh

The village is about one hour away from Ferizli and is situated in a beautiful place and consists of 60 houses. There are approximately 300 inhabitants. They have an old, decrepit wooden church dedicated to St George and one married priest named Reverend Sahag. Apparently this church owns 3,000 kurush, but this sum disappeared long ago.

The church has a school in a very poor state with about 22 pupils, taught by an ordinary bookkeeper. It is a very distressing sight.

Of the 60 houses, three are Protestant with 15 inhabitants. Protestantism has been established in the village for 15 years and the community has a meeting hall. A preacher comes from Adabazar (three hours away) to preach. It does not have a school. The local people say

---

* The word used here and throughout this survey is *tankaran* (museum) but is used to mean "meeting hall."

that, surprisingly, there has been no increase in their numbers during these last few years.

The people are generally farmers and involved with sericulture and have no morals.

Nor Kiugh*

Nor Kiugh is located in a valley about half an hour away from Tamlekh. It is a small village of 21 houses with about 100 inhabitants.

It has a small wooden church dedicated to St Garabed, whose door has been shut for a year, although before that it apparently had a married priest named Reverend Garabed from Adabazar. He left the village and returned to his birthplace to make more money, leaving the people, now without a priest, in despair.

They do have a school which is almost closed as there is not even an ordinary bookkeeper who could teach.

The people are generally farmers and involved with sericulture and mainly poor and have no morals.

This is wretched situation that a real Armenian would not be able to tolerate if he saw it.

Adabazar

Adabazar is located in a beautiful, wide plain with many mulberry trees three hours from Nor Kiugh and eight from Nicomedia. It has 3,000 houses encompassing all three nationalities – Armenian, Greek and Turkish. There are 1,300 Armenian houses in their own separate quarter with approximately 6,500 inhabitants.

They have four big, magnificent churches dedicated to the Holy Archangel, St Garabed, St Gregory the Illuminator and St Stepannos. The church of the Holy Archangel has six married priests and the others four each. The quarter is divided into four parishes, each based on a church.

Each parish has two schools; one for boys and another for girls. They also have meeting halls for grown women, where they gather, after each Sunday morning service, to hear lectures on national history† and

---

* New Village.

Christian doctrine. Each hall is run by a committee made up of six ladies who also are also trustees of the girls' schools.

The boys' schools are similarly progressive, or even more so. But each school relies on funds provided by the churches as they have no sources of income. There is also one institution like a college, whose costs are covered by the population. It has a good Armenian studies teacher[*] who is well versed in Turkish, teaching about 40 of the best pupils who, having mastered grammar, carry out translations and write essays in classical Armenian (*krapar*). They also study mathematics and a sufficiency of Turkish.

The second class of pupils are mastering the eight parts of speech.

The third class are studying the parts of speech, at the same time taking lessons in national and church history[†], thanks to the efforts of the previously mentioned teacher who is a graduate of the Armash school.

All this excludes the St Stepannos parish, which consists of 60 houses and whose school has only 60 pupils who don't receive tuition of the same quality. There is no real education for the fair sex, but they have great hopes for the future and for progress from day to day.

The people are generally merchants; some people engage in sericulture. There is great wealth through trade. The Armenians are industrious but not very rich; they are satisfied and, according to their nature, docile and obedient.

The Greeks have a separate quarter on the eastern side of the town with 300 houses. They have two churches and a school for both sexes attached to each. They are, like the Armenians, half artisans and half merchants.

The Turks are spread around the town and have four mosques and one imperial school. They have no appetite for learning, wandering in

---

† It is not clear whether this means Armenian history or that of the Ottoman Empire.

* The word used here is *haigapan*. I have used this literal translation throughout this work.

† I have used this term throughout for the author's description *srpazan badmoutiun*. This seems to have been not just church history but possibly about the saints, perhaps a little theology, church customs etc.

Egyptian darkness. They are not fanatics and live in harmony with the Christians. They are generally farmers. There are also merchants among them as well as a few artisans.

There are 30 Protestant houses among those of the Armenians. They have a meeting hall and one missionary (preacher) but have not apparently increased in numbers.

There are also about 30 houses of Tatar refugees who are farmers and artisans and are Mohammedans.

No one who is interested in the town's location can find anywhere to satisfy his curiosity as, on the eastern side, the River Sankaria (Sakaria) flows swiftly to Pontus; the water flowing into Lake Sabandja, looking like a small river is on the eastern side of the town; the River Sankaria flows past the village of Ferizli which is four hours from Adabazar. The great waterwheel is built on this river, providing water to the cisterns that distribute water to the fountains through pipes. The town has the appearance of being an island.

Geyve's Michakiugh[*]

This village, established on the summit of a mountain with panoramic views, is eight hours from Adabazar and one and a half hours to the east of Geyve. It has two communities, Armenian and Greek.[†]

The Armenians number approximately 200 families or about 1,000 individuals.

They have an ancient stone-built church dedicated to the Holy Mother of God with three married priests: leading priest (*avak kahana*) Reverend Tateos and Reverends Kapriel and Hmayag.

The church has a two-storey school for boys and girls attended by about 250 pupils, taught by a competent teacher of Armenian studies who is a graduate of Armash. There are also advanced pupils who are taught grammar and mathematics, at the same time learning church history and doctrine. The school has an ample income of 12,000 kurush, resulting in it becoming progressive.

---

[*] Michakiugh means 'middle village'
[†] The author, further on in this section, makes it clear that these people are not actual Greeks, but Armenians who profess the Greek Orthodox faith.

The majority of the Armenian population is mainly engaged in sericulture, although this year they have been subject to losses. Despite this, they are generally in a good position both economically and morally. There is still enthusiasm for study even during an unsuccessful time like the present, so they have turned all their attention on the school.

About 20 houses of people from the village are located at the foot of the mountain about an hour away, who settled there because of internecine differences a few years ago... This hamlet, called Eshme Village, has a chapel and a resident elderly married priest.

The Greeks are a community of 450 families. They have a magnificent stone-built church with a cupola and have three married priests. They number approximately 2,250 individuals and, like the Armenians, are engaged in sericulture and various forms of trade. They are called Armenian-Hroms and arrived in ancient times from Agn.

Kourdbelen

Located on the eastern side of the summit of a mountain two hours from Michakiugh, Kourdbelen has panoramic views. It has 600 houses with about 3,000 inhabitants.

It has a newly-built, huge, magnificent church with a cupola and is decorated with crosses. It is dedicated to the Holy Mother of God and has four married priests: leading priest (avak kahana) Reverend Haroutiun and Reverends Krikor, Bedros and Garabed.

The church has a school attached to it which is in a completely bad state; it doesn't even have ordinary reading classes, although the community is reasonably wealthy.

The people are artisans and involved in sericulture, but have no feelings for the school.

Kendjelar

Kendjelar is located in a hollow surrounded by hills and is one hour east of Kourdbelen. It consists of 250 houses with the population numbering approximately 1,250 individuals. They have a magnificent church dedicated to St Sarkis with four married priests: leading priest (avak kahana) Reverend Hohannes and Reverends Sarkis, Garabed and Tateos.

The church has a school for boys and girls where pupils are taught by a teacher versed in Armenian studies who is a graduate of Armash. It is quite progressive and there are pupils who are learning grammar and mathematics. The number of pupils is about 200. The school has a board of trustees which always keeps it in good state. The people are quite in favour of education.

They are farmers and involved in sericulture.

There is an ancient pilgrimage site about a quarter of an hour from this village called St Sarkis; its written history, by a miracle, is in my hands.* The foundations and main altar and the arch above it are still standing. There is a cave nearby which is only accessibly by a single person at a time with a spring of sweet-tasting water in it. There were, in the past, three statues standing at the edge of this spring and it is thought that this ruin is between 1,000 and 1,200 years old. Apparently every year, on the feast of St Sarkis, many people make a pilgrimage and visit it from various places. This is what the villagers testify to.

The people are mostly poor, with a few having middle incomes.

Sabandja or Heghinoupolis†

This village is located on the western shore of the lake about five hours distant from Kendjelar. It is a beautiful place with many fruit trees.

Its population is made up of the three races: Armenians, Greeks and Turks.

The Armenians live in a separate quarter made up of 25 houses and number about 125 individuals.

They have a small church dedicated to St Minas with a single married priest, Reverend Asdvadzadour.

The church has a school in the most wretched state which is almost closed down.

The people are few in number and have little wealth. They are lazy and slow and have no morals.

---

* One is left to wonder what happened to this account…
† This is the literal transliteration of the Armenian form of the name.

The Greeks have a quarter of 12 houses with 25 inhabitants; they have a church and school. The people are poor.

The Turks live in a separate quarter of 1,000 houses and number 3,000 individuals. They are quite wealthy and live by farming and sericulture. They have two mosques and a school, but the people are in extreme darkness.

There are several large hotels in the Turkish quarter.

There is a large lake in front of the village, which is almost impossible to walk round even in 13 hours. As the lake's water is sweet, the majority of the villagers make do with it for all purposes. It is said that at one time there were large buildings on its edge, but the lake grew larger and they disappeared beneath its surface. The lake is now called Lake Sabandja.

Aslan Bey[*]

Five hours south east of Sabandja, this village is located on a high hill and comprises 300 houses, whose population is about 1,500 people.

It has a magnificent church dedicated to the Holy Mother of God with three married priests: leading priest (avak kahana) Reverend Mardiros and Reverends Hovagim and Hovhannes.

The church has a school named Mamigonian, with about 200 pupils in which both sexes are taught by a teacher well versed in Armenian studies. The advanced pupils are taught grammar and mathematics as well as church history and Christian doctrine. This school has six trustees who cater for its needs, with income from the church supporting it as it lacks its own income. There are hopes that the school will progress now.

There is a meeting hall where the people occasionally gather as they have some interest in learning, but being subject to the recession in this poor year, they have cooled towards the school.

The usual trades are sericulture, charcoal burning and commerce. Farming has not really been started, although some people are beginning to work the land, as the village has significant areas lying fallow.

There is a silk factory in the village in which about 50 of the poorest girls are working, earning two or three kurush a day. It is a very sad sight.

---

[*] This village was later popularly known as Arslan Beg.

Ovadjek

This village is two hours distant from Aslan Bey and is located on the south eastern side of a beautiful hill at the foot of a mountain. It comprises 300 houses with about 1,500 inhabitants.

It has a magnificent large church dedicated to St Gregory the Illuminator with four married priests: leading priest (avak kahana) Reverend Garabed and Reverends Krikor, Aristages and Vrtanes.

The church has a school, in a wretched state due to the people's poverty and suffering. The number of pupils should be 150, but there are very few taking lessons. Their teacher is a person well versed in Armenian studies who is a graduate of the holy monastery of Armash. The school, not having its own income, relies on the people's purse for its upkeep and continuance, hence its wretched state.

The people are very poor and extremely lazy. Their usual trades are sericulture and farming as well as charcoal burning. They are poverty-stricken.

There are also six houses of Protestants with 30 inhabitants. They have their meeting hall and a preacher named Arakel. He also teaches the children in his school.

Deongel

Half an hour from Ovadjek, this small village of 40 houses is set in fields and gardens on the south eastern side of a beautiful small hill. Its population numbers about 200 people.

It has a church dedicated to St Sarkis with one married priest, Reverend Hagop.

The church has a school with 30 pupils taught by a bookkeeper with some knowledge of Armenian studies. It depends on the poverty-stricken people for its income.

It should be said that the priest doesn't even have a set of vestments. This situation causes real Armenian hearts great pain.

Their land is fertile but, due to the villagers' laziness, it is uncultivated.

Bardizag

About one and a half hours distant from Deongel and two hours by boat from Nicomedia, it is on a hill that runs north-south at the bottom of a

The Main Part of the Diocese of Nicomedia

large mountain named Geodagh. Bardizag is a small town[*] with 1,100 houses. Its population is approximately 6,000 people.

It has a magnificent church dedicated to St Hagop[†] with four married priests: leading priest (avak kahana) Reverend Krikor and Reverends Mgerdich, Tavit, Garabed and Hovhannes.[‡]

The church has a school for boys and girls, with about 400 pupils, of whom about 40 study grammar, mathematics, French and Turkish. They are taught by a Badveli[**] teacher versed in Armenian studies named Kevork Shirinian of Kara Hisar.

The pupils in the first class, having mastered grammar, make translations from classical (*krapar*) into modern Armenian as well as studying mathematics. They also write essays. Their French and Turkish are quite advanced.

Those in the second class, having mastered the eight parts of speech and consonance,[††] are quite advanced, but their French and Turkish is not so good.

The third class are only studying the eight parts of speech.

Lessons in church history and Christian doctrine are also given.

There is a meeting hall in the school which is used occasionally.

The school owns about 30,000 kurush worth of land, the annual profits of which are only used for the boys' school. The girls' school is in a very poor state and is considered to be practically closed due to the people's indifference, although the above-mentioned teacher has protested to the notables about it many times. But no one listens to his needs. The notables don't even give this linguist-teacher, who is well versed in Armenian studies, an adequate salary, although he is worthy of

---

[*] The word used here is kiughakaghak or village-town (small town).
[†] St James of Nisibis.
[‡] The author has named five.
[**] Badveli: "honourable" – a title usually given to Protestant preachers.
[††] I have used the word 'consonance' to express the term *hamatsaynoutiun*. This I think, in this case refers to the way the classical language has to have its parts of speech all in the same form or agreement. My interpretation may be subject to correction.

recompense, as he has worked hard for the betterment of the school. He has to farm land occasionally to provide for his family.

The people are inquisitive, but don't have any principles and are therefore lazy and morally dead. For a true Armenian, these people's inertia is death.

There is a pilgrimage site half an hour distant from this small town dedicated to St Minas where the people of the village occasionally go and pray, but I don't know its history.

The Protestants live in a separate quarter made up of 50 houses containing about 250 individuals. They have a meeting hall with a school and a preacher. Protestantism was established in this small town 20 years ago, but their numbers have not grown.

There are also about 40 houses of Roman Catholics numbering about 200 individuals. This community was founded six years ago. It has a church with a school, but both Protestants and Catholics are in a poor state.

Part 2

The Second Part of the Diocese of Nicomedia Consisting of the Armenian Villages in the Yalova Province

Shakhshakh

Shakhshakh village is three and a half hours by ship from both Constantinople and Nicomedia. It is located a quarter of the way up a small hill running north to south facing the sea opposite Dardja and comprises 80 houses with approximately 450 inhabitants.

It has a small church dedicated to St Nigoghayos with one married priest named Reverend Nigoghayos.

The church has a school with about 30 pupils – both boys and girls – and is taught by a teacher well versed in Armenian studies who is a graduate of Armash. Not having its own income, it relies on the public purse and is therefore in a very poor state. This is despite the fact that the church had, at one time, 30,000 kurush which disappeared long ago. This money had been collected with great difficulty, then handed over to a trusteeship of six individuals so that a piece of land could be bought to improve the school in the future.

The people are mainly farmers and sericulture workers and are mostly wealthy, with poor people in the minority, but they always spend their wealth to no purpose.

Kheledj Kiugh

This village is one hour distant from Shakhshakh and two hours from the seashore in a south easterly direction. It comprises 100 houses set on a small hill and has approximately 500 inhabitants.

It has a small, beautiful, stone-built church dedicated to St Sarkis with one married priest named Reverend Garabed.

The church has a school which is in a derelict state, but there are hopes that it will be rebuilt and cater for 35 pupils, who are at present taught by an ordinary bookkeeper. The church has 11,267 kurush which was collected and handed over to the school trusteeship made up of four individuals who are to buy a piece of land to bring the school an income and improve it.

The people are mainly farmers and are involved in sericulture. They have average wealth. Although both men and women are good workers, they waste their money due to their dark ignorance.

Choukhour Kiugh

One hour from Kheledj village in a south easterly direction and three hours inland from the seashore, this village is a small one of 48 houses situated among wheat fields and has a population of approximately 240 people.

It has a small church dedicated to the Holy Mother of God with one married priest named Reverend Mardiros. This priest has serious accusations levelled against him by the villagers. I conducted an examination and found that the accusations were true: instead of sowing peace, there is always discord due to his evil-nature. He apparently often punishes the people by keeping the church door closed for days on end, etc.

The church has a school which has 30 pupils who are taught by an ordinary bookkeeper. It is in a decrepit state and the teaching is without merit. The church had a capital sum of 20,134 kurush collected with difficulty from the villagers for the school. It was to be used to purchase land; the profits from it to be used for the school. A trusteeship of four people was also created to look after the school.

The people are farmers and are involved in sericulture. Although they constantly work hard, they waste what they earn.

Kartsi Kiugh

One hour distant in a south-westerly direction from Chokhour village and three hours inland from the coast, this village consists of 150 houses with a population of approximately 800 people. The village is surrounded by high hills and lies in an area of bumpy valleys, known to the Turks as Lale Dere because all the land is subject to movement.[*] The people live in

---

[*] The author means that it was subject to earth tremors and earthquakes.

their houses in a state of constant fear, especially during the winter when they face great dangers.

They have a magnificent church dedicated to the Holy Mother of God with two married priests: Reverends Nerses and Hovhannes. The latter's extreme behaviour is the reason for scandals occurring in the village.

They have a school, although it is in a decrepit state – in other words they do not even have a teacher. To rectify this situation the church had a sum of 10,438 kurush which is considered lost. It was collected from the villagers with difficulty. The school was placed under the trusteeship of four individuals and the money was to have been used to purchase some land, the annual profits of which were to go to the school for its upkeep and obviate any deficiencies.

The people are generally farmers and are involved in sericulture and are poor.

Their situation would make a genuine Armenian's heart cringe especially as they have been left without help or visits from outside. There is no doubt that they will one day fall into the claws of wolves in sheep's clothing who pursue people like them in the villages.

Chengiler

Chengiler is two hours distant south east from Kartsi village and located between Nicomedia and Lake Niceae. It has 500 houses with approximately 2,500 inhabitants.

The village has a decrepit church with five married priests: leading priest (avak kahana) Reverend Arsen, Reveverend Garabed, the learned Reverend Minas and Reverends Boghos and Hohannes.

The church only has a boys' school with 300 pupils who are taught by an ordinary bookkeeper who has no real education.

I was very upset to find that there was no girls' school, so I had one opened with the greatest difficulty, where about 250 girls are taught to read.

I took over the said church's annual income of 12,000 kurush, accrued from lands it owns, and handed it over to the schools for their repair and maintenance and had both placed under a new trusteeship of six elected individuals.

I also added 10,000 kurush the church owned (additional to the above-mentioned sum) that was collected from the villagers, to the sum quoted above.

There are four individuals who are Protestants and have their own preacher and a neat school where Armenian Apostolic families have begun to send their children, as their own (Armenian Apostolic) schools are in such a poor state. This is very saddening and shameful.

Some of the people are farmers, or are involved in sericulture, with others are artisans or merchants. They are mostly wealthy, but generally wander in the prison of darkness, so bad results are not uncommon.

The people must be provided with moral guidance as a matter of urgency.

Bazar's Medz Nor Kiugh[*]

Medz Nor Kiugh is a small town half an hour from Chengiler, four hours from the coast and an hour south east of Lake Niceae. It has 800 houses and a population of approximately 4,000 people.

It has a magnificent church dedicated to St Garabed with five married priests: leading priest (avak kahana) Reverend Boghos and Reverends Garabed, Stepan, Simon and the learned Reverend Krikor who was a student in Armash. The church's income is about 12,000 kurush which is allocated to the school.

It has a magnificent prelacy with three rooms as well as a school for boys and girls. The teacher there is the famous and meritorious teacher Hovhannes Mavian who is a graduate of Armash and a Protestant preacher (*badveli*), who has 40 pupils with another 20 selected or due to enter the senior school (*ousoumnaran*) soon.

The school is divided into three classes: the first is made up of pupils who have mastered grammar and have the ability to write essays in classical Armenian and make translations from it. They also study mathematics. They will be starting lessons in Turkish in March.[†]

The second class have mastered the eight parts of speech and are studying consonance.

---

[*] Medz Nor Kiugh: Large New Village
[†] March 1871.

The third class are studying the eight parts of speech as well as national and church history.

It has a first school (*dzaghgots*) in which about 210 children are taught.

The school has a trusteeship made up of six individuals who make every effort to look after the needs of the boys' school.

The girls' school has about 200 pupils whose 13 teachers also the make up the school's trusteeship body. The girls study grammar, Christian doctrine and national history.

Apart from all this, there is also a Selfless Union[*] which, every Sunday morning, has grown people spending their time reading in the school. There is also an Araradian Union whose aim is to assist the Selfless Union and help in the betterment of the trades' people's work and improve agriculture.

The village has considerable numbers of mulberry and olive trees as well as vineyards which satisfy their needs. They have a great source of income in the sowing of plants producing hashish.

The villagers are well off, but the majority are ignorant and lack morals.

There are 30 Turkish houses comprising approximately 270 individuals, mixed with the Armenians. They have a small mosque. They are moderately well off and live in harmony with the Armenians.

Bazar's Michakiugh

This is a village located about a quarter of an hour's distance south from Chengiler and is made up of 350 houses. The population numbers approximately 1,800.

They have magnificent church dedicated to the Holy Mother of God with three married priests: leading priest (avak kahana) Reverend Hovhannes and Reverends Garabed and Parsegh.

The church has decrepit schools for boys and girls. There are 150 pupils in the boys' school who spend their time reading. The girls' school has 40 pupils. There is a trusteeship of four individuals that looks after the progress of both schools with 1,500 kurush annual income from the

---

[*] *Antsnver Engeroutiun.*

church. The schools remain open due to further financial assistance provided by the church, as the annual sum received is not sufficient for their needs.

The majority of the people are ignorant, poor and, at the same time, extravagant. They have no moral teaching.

Some villagers are artisans, others farmers or are involved in sericulture. Some grow plants to produce hashish and a few have olive trees.

There is a mountain just behind this village named Korou that causes damage to the village and its inhabitants every year and is going to do so again soon. I can visually confirm this and the people of the village are in danger. This was also confirmed by a visiting engineer.[*]

There are 12 Turkish houses in a separate quarter that number about 60 persons. They have a ruined mosque whose minaret is a mulberry tree. They are generally farmers but are all poor. They live in harmony with the Armenians.

Bazar's Keremet

This is a small village two hours distant south east of Medz Nor Kiugh, situated at the bottom of a mountain. It has 80 houses with 400 inhabitants. A few are wealthy but the majority are poor. They are generally farmers and some are involved in sericulture.

They have a magnificent church dedicated to St Minas with two married priests: leading priest (avak kahana) Reverend Antreas and Reverend Kapriel.

They're starting to build a school for both boys and girls, but it's a poor, half-hearted effort. The hope is that with the help of the newly-elected four trustees the situation will improve and a suitable teacher will eventually be provided to teach the 40 boys and 30 girls of the village grammar, mathematics, church history, national history and music.

This village is two and a quarter hours distant from Lake Niceae and its fertile fields cover quite an area. It has many olive trees and a good quality tobacco is cultivated.

---

[*] Natanian uses the Turkish word *muhendis* here.

The Second Part of the Diocese of Nicomedia

There are 10 Turkish houses in a separate quarter with a population of about 40 individuals. They hate the Armenians they live alongside.

The Armenians are wandering in the dark prison of ignorance.

It takes 24 hours to walk round Lake Niceae or Lake Askanis as it was called, where, it is thought, there were, in the past, villages and towns. The water is very sweet and there many different kinds of fish to be found in it. A stream flows from it to Marmarina Bay.

This village is surrounded by three or four Turkish villages, whose inhabitants always hate the Armenians. Bazar's Keremet's villagers are always being persecuted by many Turks. I saw an example of this on 6th February.

There is a sulphurous flow some distance away from the village whose liquid is very beneficial.

Yalakh Derc

Located south east of Keremet on a road four hours distant, this village is set among hills and many mulberry trees and fields. It is made up of 100 houses with a population of about 500 people.

It has a magnificent small church dedicated to the Holy Archangel with two married priests: leading priest (avak kahana) Reverend Kapriel and Reverend Mikayel.

The church has a school with about 80 girls and boys who are taught by an ordinary bookkeeper. It is in a very poor state. The church has land providing an annual income of 1,500 kurush which is used for the school through a trusteeship made up of four individuals who look after the school's needs.

The church had a sum of 26,000 kurush; I wanted to find out who held it as it was considered lost.

The village has a Turk and Greek-loving tyrannical ruler (*ishkhan*) named M Haroutiun who is also a government member who has got the naive villagers in his claws for his own profit, using many merciless methods. When I began to make enquiries about the missing sum of money, this same tyrannical person, using the trustees[*] that were his creatures, initially declared unanimously that they knew nothing about it

---

[*] The author uses the Turkish word mutevelli here.

and wanted to escape from my presence. Then, through another ploy, it became clear that those same people had begun to confess that the 26,000 kurush had been left with them for years without any profit accruing for the poor people, thus usurping the villagers' rights.

This is how such merciless, tyrannical Armenians keep the people of all the villages in ignorance with their own hands.

The villagers are farmers and are involved in sericulture. Some sow plants to produce hashish.

Merdigeoz[*]

Located half an hour south east of Yalakh Dere, Merdigeoz is a small village of 100 houses with a population of approximately 500 inhabitants. It is about six hours distant from Lake Niceae and two and a half hours from Karamoursal on the coast.

The village has a magnificent small church dedicated to St Garabed with two married priests: leading priest (avak kahana) Reverend Garabed (who always has grave accusations levelled against him) and Reverend Vrtanes.

The church has a school with about 50 pupils who are taught by an ordinary bookkeeper, but it is in the worst possible state.

The people are mostly poor with only a few people having a reasonable income, apart from Reverend Garabed, who is uniquely wealthy and lends money to villagers with a percentage interest, using beastly machinations.[†] He has captured the hearts of the villagers and, using tyrannical methods, prevents the children from gaining an education.

It should also be said that in reality, holding the position of trustee, he has kept the church's accounts himself. It is not known what has happened to the church's capital of 26,000 kurush or who is holding it.

Due to the village's poverty, the widowed women and grown up girls go to the village named Karamoural, two and a half hours away, to work as servants in Turkish houses, where various bad things occasionally

---

* Later known as Merdegeoz.

† One must assume this was to enforce payment!

happen, such as when a woman accepted the Mohammedan religion quite by chance* in the recent past.

The people are farmers and are involved in sericulture; some are charcoal burners, but their greatest income is from the fruit trade.

There are also 12 Turkish houses in a separate quarter with 60 inhabitants. They are extremely poor. They have a small mosque, whose minaret is made of wood. They live in harmony with the Armenians.

---

* The word used here is *badahmamp*.

Part 3

Description of Wedding Celebrations in the Armenian-Inhabited-Villages of the Yalova Region

Betrothal, Inter-family Relationships and Marriage

Betrothal

When a family's son has come of age, his parents begin to look around and ask about a prospective bride for him. This duty, in the first instance, is undertaken by the young man's mother.

When she receives information that a this or that family has a little girl of eight to ten years old – I use the word little girl (*oriortig*) as someone of this age is generally known as a child or little girl and not 'young lady' (*oriort*) – she informs her superior, in other words the boy's father and negotiations immediately begin between the two sides. The boy's father talks of his income and love of brilliant metals, not about the boy's thoughtfulness or good character.

Both sides, on the following day, go to the church office and there, in the presence of the priests and seat-holder,* the girl's family carries out their part of the betrothal ceremony, presenting a three-*gankoun*† length of material (to the boy's family). In return, his family gives the girl's family a piece of cloth with a ring tied to one of its corners. The ceremony ends with toasts of glasses of *oghi* being drunk.

People come to the boy's father's house that same evening to offer congratulations. The number of people arriving gradually becomes much greater and a huge cloth is spread in the centre. First, prepared food is brought in, followed by bottles of wine. People become tipsy after drinking considerable quantities of wine, with animated conversations taking place, resulting in people wanting music to be played – with one wanting a musical instrument, another a drum – eventually everyone is satisfied and the enjoyable party continues. After bowing to Bacchus' picture many times, the party breaks up at about ten or eleven o'clock the

---

* This Armenian term is not understood.
† Approximately 4 feet 6 inches or 135cm.

following morning. This continues for ten or twelve days, followed by the "establishment of relations."

Inter-family relationships

The boy's father hires a drumming herald (*munedik*) to go to his relatives and announce that "we are going to see the prospective bride this evening, please attend." Thus between 10 and 25 householders assemble, taking with them half a sheep and about 20 large frying-pans' worth of pastries.

This mixed crowd of men and women goes to the girl's father's house. He and his family have already got about the same number of visitors – making a total of between 40 and 50 householders and their families present.

After eating and drinking well, which is no different from constructing the Tower of Babel, the little girl, led by someone, enters to begin to kiss the guests' hands. As she kisses each person's hand, they present her with a gift of money – 100, 250 or a little less[*] – according to their means.

After considerable time has passed eating, drinking and wasting much money on the musicians, the party begins to break up in the morning, leaving every kind of embarrassment as a souvenir.

It is then necessary for the little girl's parents to go and meet the prospective bridegroom. This takes place in exactly the same way; a big crowd with the obligatory half sheep and pastries makes its way to the boy's parents' house, where much drunkenness and debauchery may be seen. The same ceremony of "kissing of hands" begins; after he has kissed all the men's hands, the prospective bridegroom moves on to the women present who, according to their means, present him with a whole or half a bolt of cloth each.[†] Considering that insufficient, they begin to give him material suitable for overcoats (*choukhas*).

---

[*] No monetary denomination is quoted in the text – it could be paras or kurush.

[†] The word used here is *khoumash*.

Description of Wedding Celebrations

I've no idea what they will produce next in the future! This "hand kissing" is repeated several times by the girl's family that brings generous quantities of sweets and other things for the groom.

While the women victoriously do all this, the men continue their celebrations with many glasses of wine. After staying for some considerable time (on each occasion) and getting completely drunk[*] they call an end to the festivities.

These later mutual visits (cementing relations between the families) sometimes takes place, but not with the same emphasis as on the first occasion.

Marriage

The *danesh*[†] happens a year or two after the betrothal, two weeks before the wedding.[‡] About ten householders on the groom's father's side convene then go to the bride-to-be's[**] house as they did during the engagement celebrations. The bride's father has also brought approximately the same number of householders to his house.

After much jollity by all present, the haggling over the bride-to-be begins. Thanks to a well-wisher from each side, it is completed amicably with the sum of one or two white medjidies[††] being agreed. The people present then disperse.

A considerable number of women gather in the bride-to-be's house early the next morning and. after playing various games and jokes, dress the little girl in white and begin to take her from one house to another. They do this every day for two weeks, until the day comes that the groom's father begins the wedding preparations in earnest.

Musicians are hired by the groom's family from the Thursday; the groom's friends begin to assemble on that same evening. The young men enjoy themselves and the party lasts until it reaches its climax on the

---

[*] The expression used here is "having lost their drunken noses and mouths…"
[†] I believe this term means "consultation."
[‡] The bride-to-be is between 9 and 12 years old at this point.
[**] I have used this term as "littler girl," "bride-to-be" etc. are used indiscriminately.
[††] "White medjidie" means a silver coin of a particular value.

Saturday, when the groom and a few friends begin going from house to house.

They have drinks at each house; other young men join them and so a large crowd finally arrives at the groom's father's house. There they eat and drink with great gusto making much noise, with the poor groom having to go from one group to another, hoping that scuffles or fights won't break out.

The groups of young men, becoming hot-headed with drink, begin to compete and verbally abuse each other and fights do break out. It is as if a war has started; the battle lasts until dawn breaks. Then, led by the musicians, they all go to the bath house and, after much horseplay, leave and go to the godfather's house.

The godfather has already made his preparations; the young men who have come from the bath house begin to eat at his house and drink and jump up and down like monkeys. After being there for some considerable time, they leave and go back to the groom's house.

They then go to the barber's shop to be shaved; I'll refrain from describing the young men's antics there.

After this, they return to the groom's house, where the group of young men and young women prepare to go to the bride's house to bless the *halaf** accompanied by musicians. The priest (*kahana*) arrives to carry out the blessing and, having done so, leaves. The musicians resume playing and some young women and the young bride begin dancing in pairs, surrounded by the crowd. The celebration thus ends and the crowd leaves.

The crowd returns directly to the groom's house, having seen the bride; they then ceremoniously dress the groom.

That evening a huge crowd of women and girls, accompanied by some young men and led by the musicians, go to the bride's house for the "henna"† celebration. It is another scene of disgraceful antics. First the girls dance in pairs then they play with the henna itself. After this the crowd of women and girls call for the game called "something squeezed into the golden cup" (*alten tas ichinde knam ezildi*) to be played. Then

---

* Term not understood.
† The bride is adorned with henna patterns painted on her skin.

Description of Wedding Celebrations

they paint the bride-to-be with henna and the celebration ends after lasting for two hours.

The whole crowd then goes to the groom's house at three o'clock,* singing the canticle *Khorhourt khorin*,† to carry out the ceremony of dressing the bridegroom. Exactly the same scene takes place, with a mixed company of people, as on the previous day.

The crowd, as dawn breaks, prepare to go to "get the bride." They go to the little girl's house, where ladies, representing the bridegroom, have already veiled her. When this has been completed, the crowd start firing their guns – causing not a few injuries on the way – and take the bride and groom to the church. They pass through the marketplace, accompanied by the musicians with, perhaps, 20 or 30 groups doing the same.‡

The wedding guests, while the marriage is being solemnised in the church, begin four or five hours of celebrations in the form of drinking oghi and jumping about like monkeys. It is impossible, in these pages, to describe the number of shameful things that take place – fights, the use of expletives and so forth. This is how marriage celebrations end.

The bride and groom leave the church and the crowd takes them through the entire village until, finally, they all reach the groom's house. There the crowd, having filled the house, demands that the ceremonious circle dance (*khalad*) be started.

Each person present gives the young bride or the groom either a cloth, handkerchief or some other gift. After this is done, they all go up** and, after large cloths are laid in the centre, gather round them to drink and eat harisa and other foods that are provided, as if they are all starved. They enjoy themselves with stupid games while they are eating.

They then have to leave to go to a place where they can indulge in competitions (*yaresh*). When these too are completed, someone sent by the bride's mother arrives to invite the groom and his young friends to her

---

* This is Turkish time and is sometime in the late evening.
† Deep thought.
‡ This implies that several (possibly '20 or 30') marriages might have taken place at the same time in church on the same day.
** Where they go to is not made clear in the original text.

house. There they once more resume feasting and playing games and, after many disgraceful scenes, the party ends.

The evening's costs, like those of the previous one, for food etc., both have to be paid. So two sets of costs have to be met which are the groom's responsibility. So that evening the guests arrive to perform the ceremony of presenting gifts.

Several young men sent by the groom and accompanied by musicians, go to the bride's house and get her father and other people that have been invited and bring them to the groom's house accompanied by the musicians. These guests bring many copper vessels to give as presents to the bride.

Other guests arrive to do the same for the groom – also with musicians. They sit apart from those of the bride. After enjoying "Bachus' incense" for a time, the battle between the two orchestras begins and, after them playing many reprehensible pieces that are beyond human amazement, they begin to present their gifts and gradually leave.

The groom, taking a few of his friends with him, then makes his way to the godfather's house, led by the musicians. They stay awake there for the whole night, playing stupid games. They return to the wedding house (the groom's) to eat khash ceremoniously.

After eating and drinking all day, they then make their preparations to fetch everyone else who hadn't brought gifts the previous day that evening. The previous evening's merriment takes place once more – this being the last shameful party.

Bibliography

Minas Kasabian, *The Armenians in the Province of Nicomedia*, Azadamard Press, Bardizag, 1913. (In Armenian).

Krikor Mkhalian, *Bardizag and its People*, translated by Ara Stepan Melkonian, Gomidas Institute, London 2014

www.ingramcontent.com/pod-product-compliance
Lightning Source LLC
Chambersburg PA
CBHW051719040426
42446CB00008B/968